The Story of Coding

By James Floyd Kelly

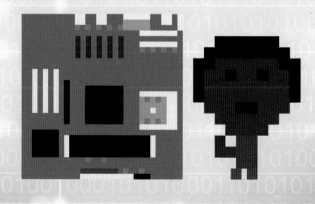

Senior Editor Caryn Jenner
Editor Radhika Haswani
Project Art Editor Yamini Panwar
Art Editors Emma Hobson, Kanika Kalra, Rashika Kachroo
Jacket Editor Francesca Young
Jacket Designers Dheeraj Arora, Amy Keast
DTP Designer Dheeraj Singh
Sr. DTP Designer Jagtar Singh
Picture Researcher Sakshi Saluja
Producer, Pre-Production Nadine King
Producer Niamh Tierney
Managing Editor Laura Gilbert
Deputy Managing Editor Vineetha Mokkil
Managing Art Editors Neha Ahuja Chowdhry, Diane Peyton Jones
Art Director Martin Wilson
Publisher Sarah Larter

Reading Consultant Jacqueline Harris

First published in Great Britain in 2017
by Dorling Kindersley Limited
80 Strand, London, WC2R 0RL

Copyright © 2017 Dorling Kindersley Limited
A Penguin Random House Company
17 18 19 20 21 10 9 8 7 6 5 4 3 2 1
001—298983—Jun/17

A CIP catalogue record for this book is available from the British Library.

ISBN: 978-0-2412-8498-8

Printed and bound in China.

The publisher would like to thank the following for their kind permission to reproduce their photographs:
(Key: a-above; b-below/bottom; c-centre; f-far; l-left; r-right; t-top)
1 **Dreamstime.com**: Boris Zatserkovnyy. 4 **123RF.com**: scanrail (b). 6 **Dreamstime.com**: Sashkinw (b). 7 **Dreamstime.com**: Vera
Volkova. 8 **123RF.com**: backgroundstore (b). 10 **123RF.com**: cobalt (b); wojciech kaczkowski (ca). 11 **Dreamstime.com**: Anton
Samsonov / iPod is a trademark of Apple Inc., registered in the U.S. and other countries (t); hxdyl (b). 12 **Dorling Kindersley**: The
Science Museum, London (br). 13 **Alamy Stock Photo**: Soberka Richard / Hemis.fr (t). John McLinden: (br). 14 **Alamy Stock Photo**:
IanDagnall Computing (cra); Photo Researchers (tl). 15 **Getty Images**: Science & Society Picture Library (cb). 16 **Alamy Stock
Photo**: INTERFOTO (tl). 17 **Science Photo Library**: James King-Holmes / Bletchley Park Trust. 18–19 **Getty Images**: Historical (b).
19 **Alamy Stock Photo**: Marek Kosmal (cr). 20 **Science Photo Library**: Earl Scott (b). 21 **123RF.com**: Maxim Basinski (bl).
Alamy Stock Photo: B Christopher (tc). **Getty Images**: Science & Society Picture Library (cr). 22 **Dreamstime.com**: Durkworx (br).
23 **Alamy Stock Photo**: Stefan Sollfors (cl). **Dreamstime.com**: Maciek905 (bl). 25 **Alamy Stock Photo**: Erik Tham (c). 31 **123RF.
com**: Wavebreak Media Ltd (cb). **Alamy Stock Photo**: MIKA Images (t). 32–33 **Dreamstime.com**: Wavebreakmedia Ltd (b).
37 **Alamy Stock Photo**: Stephen Lam (br). 38–39 **Getty Images**: Andrew Burton (b)

Jacket images: Front: 123RF.com: Andrey KOTKO, scanrail cb

All other images © Dorling Kindersley
For further information see: www.dkimages.com

A WORLD OF IDEAS:
SEE ALL THERE IS TO KNOW

www.dk.com

Contents

Words in **bold** appear in the glossary.

Chapter 1

What is Coding?

The modern world is full of computers! There are desktops, laptops, and tablets. Even a mobile phone is a mini computer.

Other **devices** have computers, too. **Satellites** in space are controlled by computers. Modern TVs and washing machines also have computers. Modern cars have them, too.

The parts of a device that you can touch are called hardware. The program that tells a computer what to do is software. Hardware and software work together.

For example, a lift is hardware. Press the button for your floor, and the software program tells the lift where to go.

Computer programs are called code. Code is a set of instructions for a computer to follow.

```
▶<head>…</head>
▼<body class=" customize-support">
 ▼<div class="wrapper">
  ▶<header>…</header>
  ▶<div id="loading-zone" class>…</div>
  ▶<div id="content" class="mod centered homepa
  ▶<div id="landscape-image-magnifier" style="d
  ▶<div id="landscape-image-magnifier" style="di
   <div class="push"></div>
  </div>
  ▶<footer class="footer">…</footer>
   <script type="text/javascript"> Cufon.now(); </s
   <script type="text/javascript" src="http://backg
  ▶<script type="text/javascript">…</script>
  ▶<div id="wpadminbar" class role="navigation">…</d
 </body>
html>
```

Code on a computer screen

Coding is writing step-by-step instructions for a computer. For example, here are instructions for a lift.

1. Wait for doors to close.

2. Wait for button to be pressed.

If button pressed is higher than current floor, move upwards.

If button pressed is lower than current floor, move downwards.

3. When current floor is the same as button pressed, open doors.

Computers Everywhere

Computer coding is used for many different things.

Global Positioning Systems (GPS)

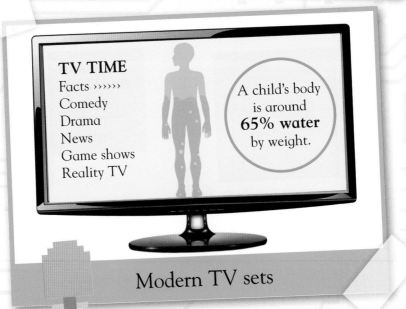

TV TIME
Facts ›››››
Comedy
Drama
News
Game shows
Reality TV

A child's body is around **65% water** by weight.

Modern TV sets

Making books

Aeroplane controls

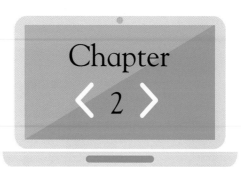

Chapter ⟨ 2 ⟩

Early Computers

The abacus is sometimes called the first computer. It was invented more than 2,000 years ago to help with maths.

Old Chinese abacus

The loom weaves a pattern shown by a punch card.

A loom weaves thread into cloth. In 1801, French weaver Joseph Jacquard made punch cards with holes for his loom. The holes told the loom how to weave patterns in the cloth. These holes were an early computer code.

Punch card

Charles Babbage

Ada Lovelace

In the mid-1800s, Charles Babbage invented the Analytical Engine to do maths problems. His friend, Ada Lovelace, wrote step-by-step programs for the Analytical Engine.

She is known as the world's first computer programmer. Lovelace realised that computers could do lots of different **tasks**.

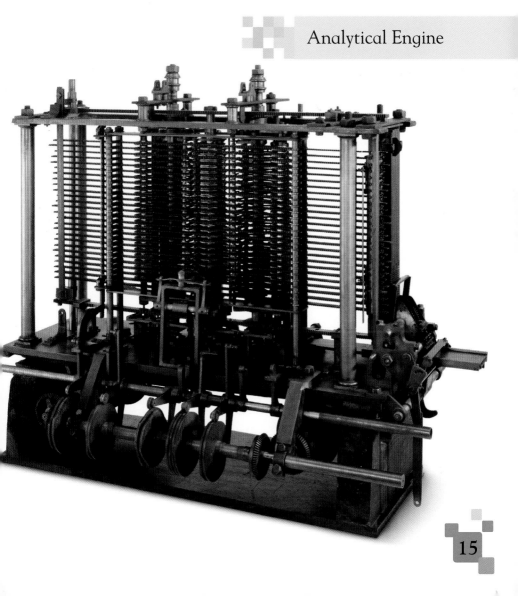

Analytical Engine

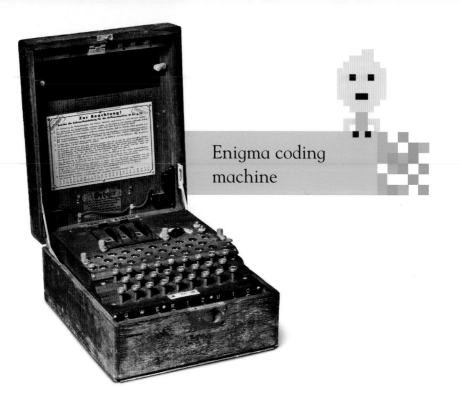

Enigma coding machine

During World War II (1939–1945), German forces used a secret code called Enigma. Countries fighting against Germany needed to work out the Enigma code to get important information. British scientist Alan Turing invented a computer that decoded Enigma and helped to end the war.

Turing's computer was called the Bombe.

ENIAC was the first computer that could be programmed to do different tasks. ENIAC was so big, it took up the space of a whole room!

Operators programmed ENIAC by putting plugs into large boards.

Since then, computers have become smaller and smaller. Now, small devices such as mobile phones use tiny **computer chips**.

Modern computer chip

Past and Present

See how computers have changed!

FACT!

In 1947, a moth trapped in a computer caused the computer to make mistakes. It was the first computer bug!

1960s

1970s

1980s

NOW

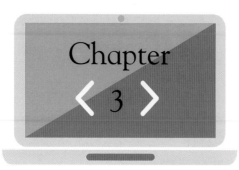

Chapter ‹ 3 ›

Coding Languages

People around the world
speak different languages.

Python code

```
# Ghost Game
from random import randint
print('Ghost Game')
feeling_brave = True
score = 0
while feeling_brave:
    ghost_door = randint(1, 3)
    print('Three doors ahead...')
    print('A ghost behind one.')
    print('Which door do you open?')
    door = input('1, 2, or 3?')
```

Javascript
code

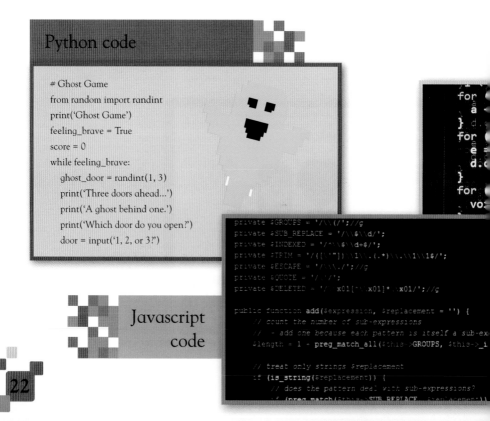

Computers have different languages, too. A computer coder needs to use a language that the computer understands.

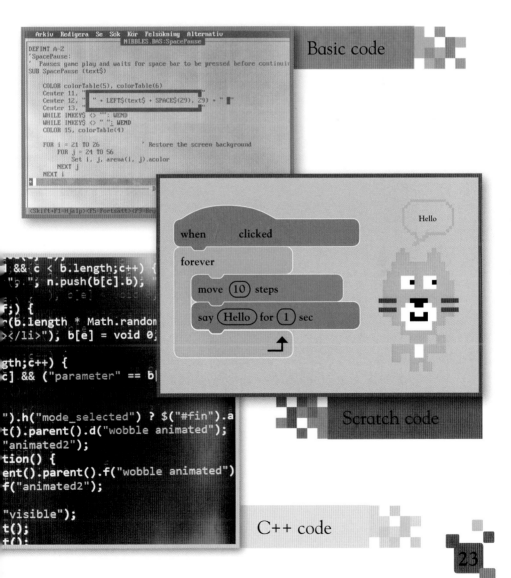

Basic code

Scratch code

C++ code

One of the simplest coding languages is "binary". Binary is made up of 1s and 0s. Different arrangements of 1s and 0s give the computer different instructions.

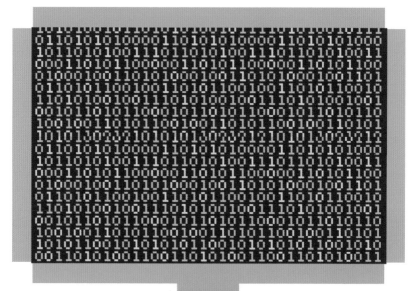

Computers use binary code to send, receive and store information.

The holes in a punch card give the computer instructions.

Punched hole

Binary code is similar to punch cards with different arrangements of holes. Punch cards were used to **input** coding until the 1970s.

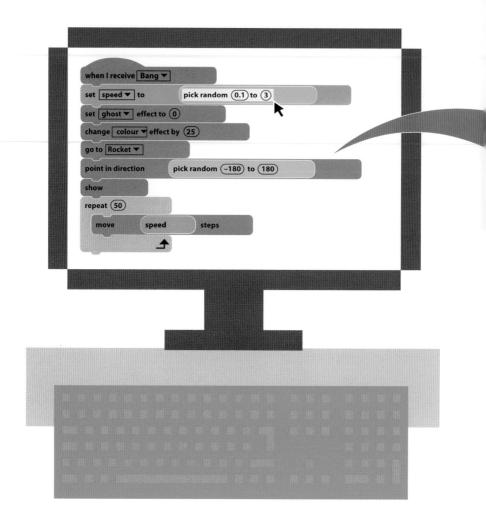

More powerful computers and better software led to new coding languages. Coders type short commands on the keyboard instead of 1s and 0s.

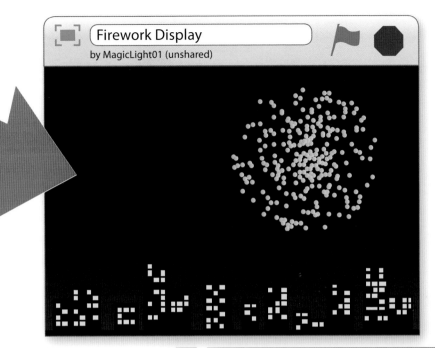

Firework Display
by MagicLight01 (unshared)

The code on the screen created this firework display.

Over time, most computer languages have become quicker and easier. Now, many pieces of code are **pre-programmed**. Coders click on pieces of code. Then they put the pieces of code together to create a whole new program.

You may have noticed that many **website** names begin with "www". It stands for "World Wide Web".

The **Internet** is a network that has linked computers since the 1960s. Then, in 1989, Tim Berners-Lee invented the World Wide Web. People all over the world started using the Internet to share information on websites. Today, there are millions of websites on the Internet.

Children around the world can learn
fun facts on Internet websites.

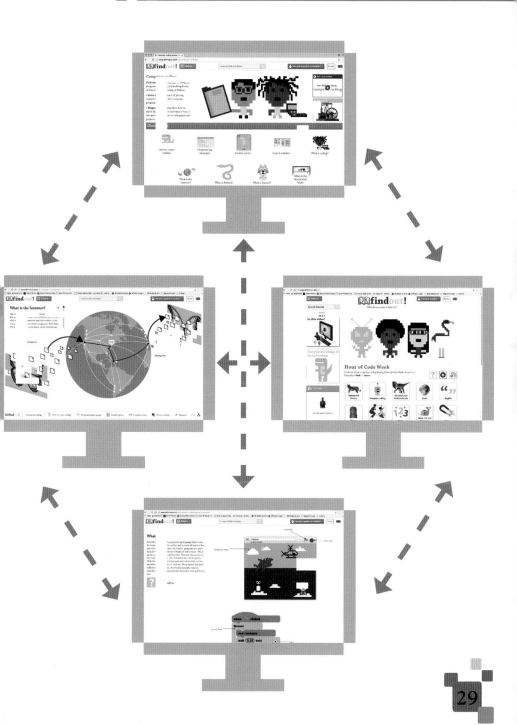

Different Uses

Different coding languages are needed to create codes for different uses. Here are a few.

Coding languages are used to create programs that help children learn.

Coding languages are used to create programs for different types of work.

Coding languages are used to create programs for scientists.

Chapter 4

Coding Today

A modern computer program is called an app. App is short for application.

Apps are easy to **download** onto small computer devices such as mobile phones and tablets. With apps, you can carry facts and fun with you all the time!

Many children enjoy using apps just as much as adults do – or maybe even more!

Apps have many different uses. People can play games and music with apps. They can edit photos and videos. Even shopping can be done with apps on the Internet.

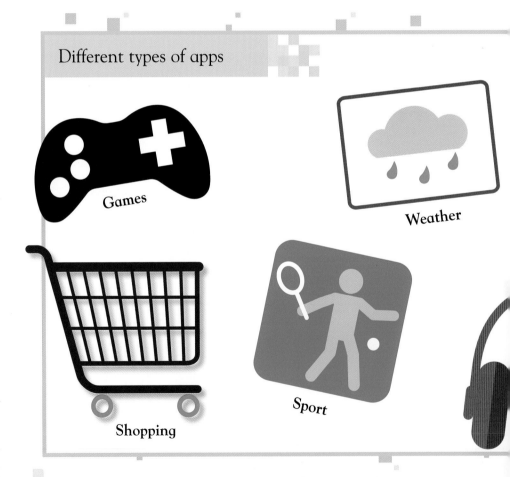

Different types of apps

Games

Weather

Shopping

Sport

People can keep in touch with messaging apps or video calls. They can find out about the weather. There are even apps that help create new apps.

Camera

Messaging

Holidays

Music

Video

All programs need code in order to work. Coding languages, such as Scratch and Python, are easy for everyone to use.

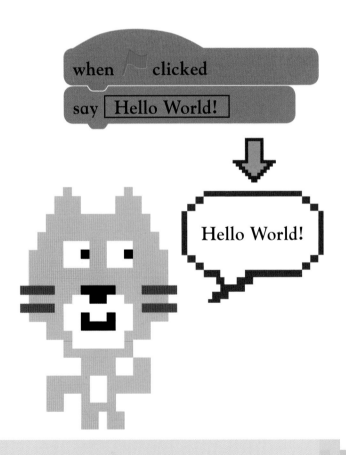

Scratch is perfect for learning how to code.

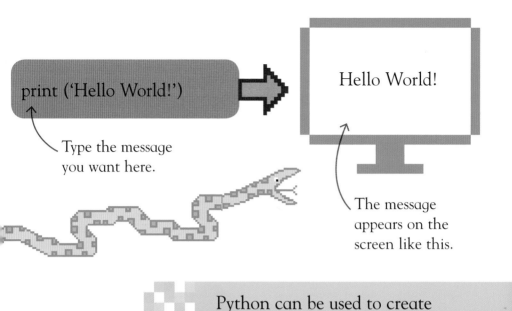

print ('Hello World!')

Type the message you want here.

Hello World!

The message appears on the screen like this.

Python can be used to create different types of programs.

These days, anyone can code! Anvitha Vijay from Australia was seven years old when she started creating apps. Her apps for children have had thousands of downloads.

Anvitha Vijay

Coding can be a fun hobby or an interesting job. Today, children even learn coding at school.

Children in coding club

There are coding clubs and camps, too. One thing is for sure – the ideas for coding are endless!

Scratch Coding

Coders can create games and **animations** with Scratch.

Click on the green flag to run the program.

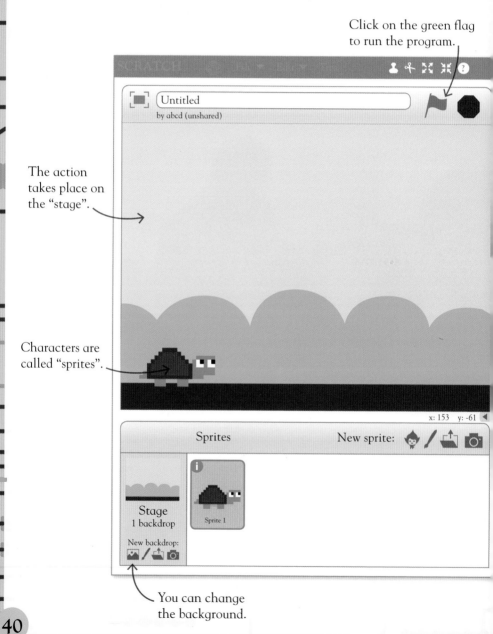

The action takes place on the "stage".

Characters are called "sprites".

SCRATCH

Untitled
by abcd (unshared)

x: 153   y: -61

Sprites

New sprite:

Stage
1 backdrop

Sprite 1

New backdrop:

You can change the background.

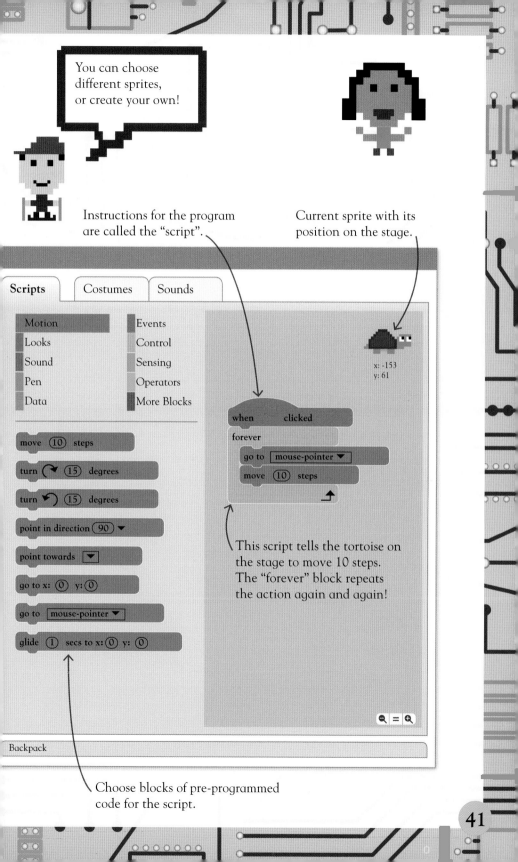

You can choose different sprites, or create your own!

Instructions for the program are called the "script".

Current sprite with its position on the stage.

Scripts | Costumes | Sounds

Motion
Looks
Sound
Pen
Data

Events
Control
Sensing
Operators
More Blocks

x: -153
y: 61

move (10) steps

turn ↻ (15) degrees

turn ↺ (15) degrees

point in direction (90) ▼

point towards ▼

go to x: (0) y: (0)

go to mouse-pointer ▼

glide (1) secs to x: (0) y: (0)

when clicked
forever
  go to mouse-pointer ▼
  move (10) steps

This script tells the tortoise on the stage to move 10 steps. The "forever" block repeats the action again and again!

Backpack

Choose blocks of pre-programmed code for the script.

41

Coding Tips

Practise creating different codes.

Try working as a team and sharing ideas with your friends.

Learn new skills at a coding club, class or camp.

Experiment! Keep trying and don't be afraid to make mistakes.

Coding Quiz

1 Is the program that tells a computer what to do called "hardware" or "software"?

2 Who is known as the world's first computer programmer?

3 Which early computer language is made up of 1s and 0s?

4 What does "www" stand for at the beginning of a website name?

5 What is the word "app" short for?

Answers on page 45

Glossary

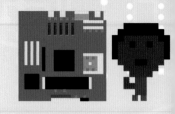

animations
moving images or graphics created
by a computer

computer chips
small electronic circuits used
in computers

devices
machines used for a particular purpose

download
send a computer file from one
computer to another

ENIAC
Electronic Numerical Integrator
and Computer

input
put information into a computer

Internet
huge network linking computers around the world

pre-programmed
coded in advance, ready to use

satellites
devices orbiting the Earth, used to send and receive information

tasks
types of work

website
location on the World Wide Web with linked pages

Guide for Parents

DK Readers is an exciting four-level reading series for children that will help to develop the habit of reading widely for both pleasure and information. These chapter books have an engaging main narrative to suit your child's reading ability, interspersed with additional information spreads in a range of reading genres. Each book is designed to develop your child's reading skills, fluency, grammar awareness, and comprehension in order to build confidence and pleasure in reading.

Ready for a *Beginning to Read* book
YOUR CHILD SHOULD

- be using phonics, including consonant blends, such as br, sp and st, to sound out unfamiliar words; and be familiar with common word endings, such as plurals, ing, ed, and ly.

- be using the meaning of the text, the grammar of a sentence, plus clues from the illustrations to check and correct his/her own reading.

- be pausing briefly at commas, and for longer at full stops; and altering his/her expression for question, exclamation, and speech marks.

A VALUABLE AND SHARED READING EXPERIENCE

For many children, reading requires a lot of effort, but adult participation can make this both fun and easier. So here are a few tips on how to use this book with your child.

TIP 1 Check out the contents together before your child begins:

- read the text about the book on the back cover.

- read through and discuss the contents page together to heighten your child's interest and expectation.

- have a brief discussion about unfamiliar or difficult words on each page.

- chat about the non-fiction reading features used in the book, such as headings, captions, and labels.

TIP 2 Support your child as he/she reads each page:

- give the book to your child to read and turn the pages.

- where necessary, encourage your child to break a word into syllables, sound out each one, and then flow the syllables together. Ask him/her to reread the sentence to check the meaning.

- you may need to help read some topic-related vocabulary and other words that may be difficult for your child.

- when there's a question mark or an exclamation mark, encourage your child to vary his/her voice as he/she reads the sentence. Demonstrate how to do this if it is helpful.

TIP 3 Praise, share, and chat:

- the additional information spreads are designed to be shared and discussed with your child. These spreads tend to be more difficult than the main narrative.

- ask your child questions about the meaning of the text and of the words used. This will help to develop comprehension skills and awareness of the language used.

A FEW ADDITIONAL TIPS

- Encourage your child to try reading difficult words by themselves. Praise any self-corrections, for example, "I like the way you sounded out that word and then changed the way you said it to make sense."

- Try to read together every day. Reading little and often is best. These books are divided into manageable chapters for one reading session. However, after 10 minutes, only keep going if your child wants to read on.

- Read a variety of books of different types with your child for pleasure and information. Reading aloud to your child is a great way to develop his or her reading skills!

- Make reading an enjoyable experience for your child.

Index